LOOKING
INSIDE
THE
Ron
Schultz
BRAIN

I L L U S T R A T E D   B Y

Peter Aschwanden

and

Nick Gadbois

John Muir Publications
Santa Fe, New Mexico

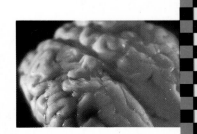

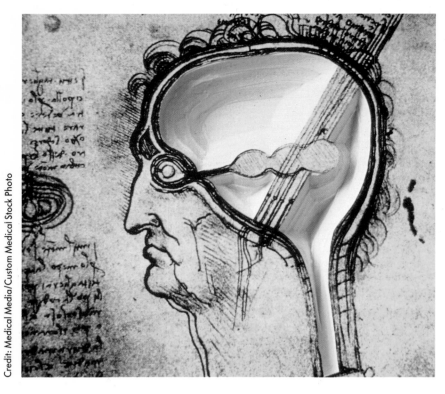

Leonardo da Vinci's famous drawing of the upper domed part of the skull

John Muir Publications, P.O. Box 613, Santa Fe, NM 87504

First edition. First printing June 1992

Library of Congress Cataloging-in-Publication Data

Schultz, Ron (Ronald), 1951—
    Looking inside the brain / Ron Schultz — 1st ed.
      p. cm. — (X-ray vision)
    Summary: Describes the anatomy and function of the brain and
discusses the senses, memory, brain diseases, and more.
    ISBN (invalid) 1-56261-046-3. — ISBN 1-56261-064-3 (pbk.)
    1. Brain—Juvenile literature. [1. Brain.] I. Title.
II. Series.
QP376.S36   1992
612.8'2—dc20   91-44927
                                                         CIP
                                                           AC

Distributed to the book trade by
W.W. Norton & Company, Inc.
New York, New York

Design: Sally Blakemore
Illustrations: Peter Aschwanden, Nick Gadbois
Typeface: Maximal, Univers
Typography: Copygraphics, Inc.
Printer: Inland Press

CONTENTS

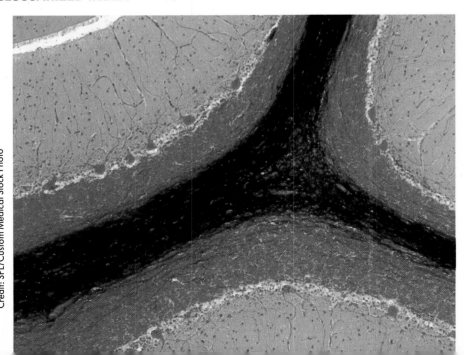

Credit: SPL/Custom Medical Stock Photo

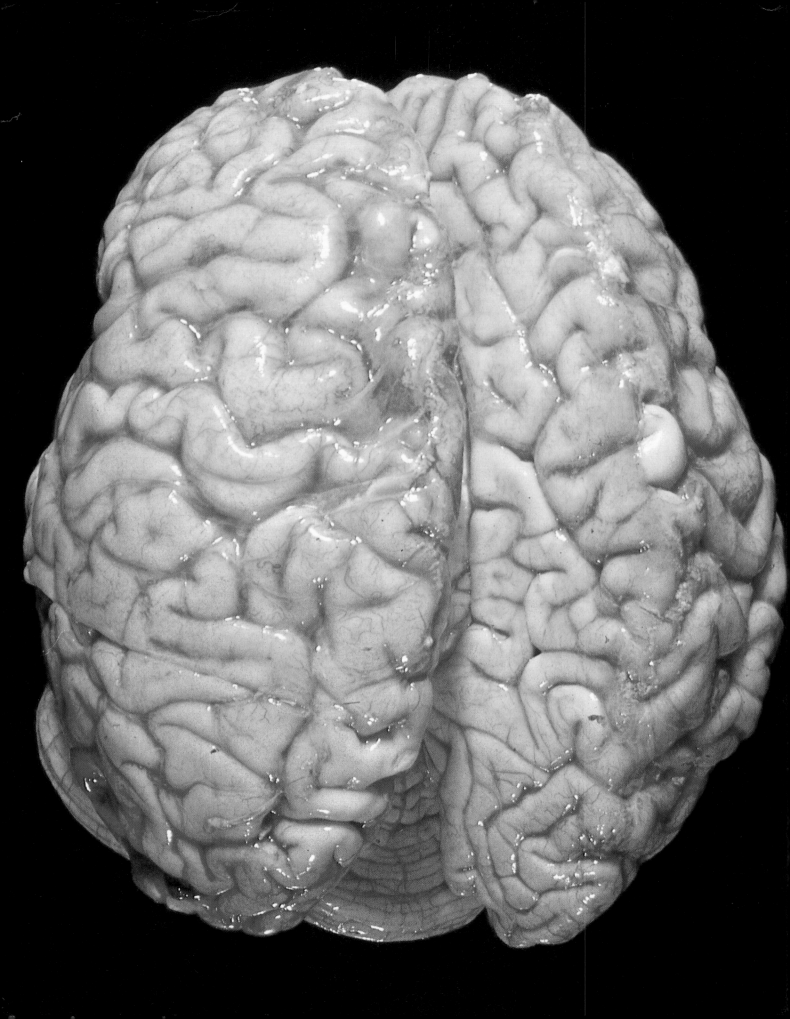

INTRODUCTION

NICK GADBOIS

FASTER THAN A SPEEDING COMPUTER, more powerful than the strongest of bodies, able to leap vast concepts in a single bound. Look! Up in your head. It's the cerebral cortex, the hypothalamus, the medulla oblongata. It's your brain!

Controlling every human activity, the brain operates 24 hours a day and on weekends, too. It makes it possible for us to hear the latest tunes, see outrageous colors, smell fantastic flowers, taste scrumptious chocolate, and touch the drippiest slime. It allows us to speak, walk, ride a skateboard, paint a picture, remember how many home runs Babe Ruth hit, feel happy, dream, and do something only humans do, wonder about the world around us. Amazingly, under "normal" circumstances, the brain does most of these things all by itself, without requiring any conscious effort on our part.

The inner workings of the brain are astonishing. Crammed into 2½ pounds of gooey, jellolike matter is an awesome organization of crisscrossing neural, or brain cell, pathways, avenues, freeways, and runways that rocket information around the body using electrochemical energy as its fuel. Stub a toe, and the pain is felt almost immediately. Hear a funny joke, and laughter comes pouring out. Trip over a sprinkler head, and a hand automatically goes up to break the fall to the ground. How the control tower we call the brain takes care of us is the story we are about to unravel.

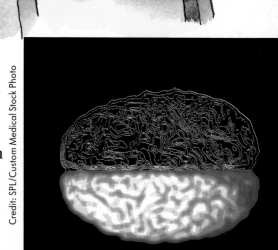

Ganglia, Glands, and

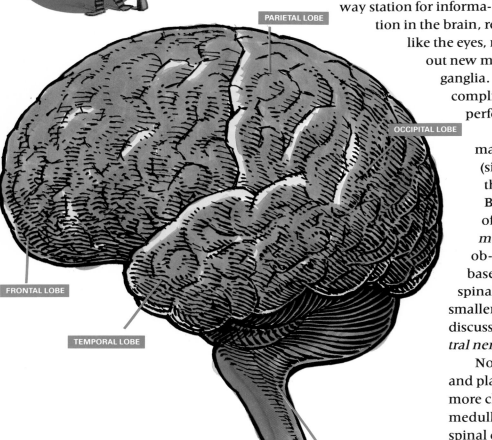

UR STORY BEGINS with a cast of characters—the major players that make up the brain team.

The brain is composed of over one hundred billion nerve cells called *neurons*. (One hundred billion is close to the number of stars in our Milky Way galaxy.) These neurons join together to form the complex glands, ganglia, and organs of the brain. *Glands* in the brain release hormones or chemical messengers that are vital to the rest of the body. *Ganglia* are tightly packed nerve cells that act as a way station for information in the brain, receiving messages from places like the eyes, nose, or tongue and then sending out new messages to muscles or other ganglia. Brain *organs* are larger and more complicated groupings of neurons that perform more complex jobs.

The brain is divided into four major playing areas: the *cerebrum* (sir-EE-brum), which is the top of the brain; the *cerebellum* (sar-a-BELL-um), which is the back part of the brain; and the *pons* and *medulla oblongata* (me-DUHL-a ob-lon-GAHT-ah), which form the base of the brain. Together with the spinal cord, these parts and a few other smaller cerebral areas, which we will discuss, make up what is called the *central nervous system*.

Now that we know the major players and playing fields, let's look a little more closely at just what they do. The medulla oblongata is at the top of the spinal cord. It's about the size of a Ping-Pong ball. On the outside, this organ looks just like a swollen part of the spinal cord. But inside, it's packed with nerve highways and two large ropes of

PARIETAL LOBE

OCCIPITAL LOBE

FRONTAL LOBE

TEMPORAL LOBE

BRAIN STEM

ANTERIOR   POSTERIOR

Organs

fibers from the left and right halves (hemispheres) of the cerebrum. These ropes control many of our voluntary body movements, like picking up a fork to eat or kicking a ball in front of us. These bundles of brain fibers also cross over to the opposite side of the medulla, which explains why the left side of the brain controls the right side of the body and the right side of the brain controls the left side of the body. Other areas in the medulla oblongata govern indispensable nonvoluntary movements like breathing, swallowing, digestion, and the beating of the heart.

Arching like a bridge just above the medulla is the pons, which actually means bridge in Latin. It is made up of a massive number of nerve fibers that start in the cerebrum and continue to the cerebellum. This connection allows us to perform skilled feats that

require visual, auditory (hearing), and muscular coordination. (It is strictly coincidence that the pons, an organ, controls activities that make it possible for us to play a musical instrument.) In addition, the pons contains the cranial nerve that turns the eyeball outward (which, of

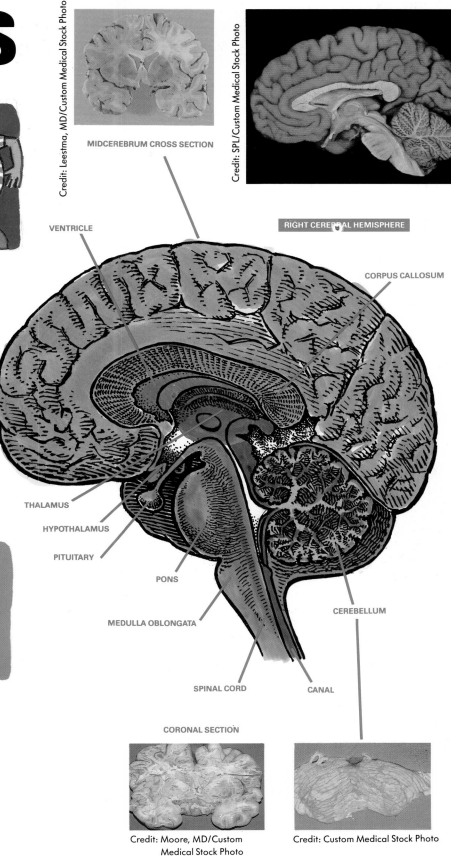

Credit: Leestma, MD/Custom Medical Stock Photo

MIDCEREBRUM CROSS SECTION

Credit: SPL/Custom Medical Stock Photo

RIGHT CEREBRAL HEMISPHERE

VENTRICLE

CORPUS CALLOSUM

THALAMUS

HYPOTHALAMUS

PITUITARY

PONS

MEDULLA OBLONGATA

CEREBELLUM

SPINAL CORD

CANAL

CORONAL SECTION

Credit: Moore, MD/Custom Medical Stock Photo

Credit: Custom Medical Stock Photo

course, makes reading music easier, too). The pons together with the medulla oblongata make up what is called the *brain stem*.

The cerebellum lies at the back of the skull and is second only in size to the cerebrum. It is about the size of your fist. Like the cerebrum, the cerebellum is very wrinkled. It looks like the outside of a walnut. Also like the cerebrum, the cerebellum is covered in gray matter, which is made up of nerve cell bodies. The inside of the cerebellum is white matter, which is made up of closely packed nerve fibers. The white matter looks very much like the veins of a leaf.

If you were a tightrope walker, the cerebellum would be a very important part of the brain for you, because it allows different muscles to work together at the same time. For example, if your cerebellum had been removed and you tried to

HAND/EYE COORDINATION

walk along a tightrope, you'd probably misjudge the position of the rope and try to put your foot down far beyond your target. Thanks to a properly functioning cerebellum, you won't shake hands too hard, stick a toothbrush too far into your mouth, or miss the handle on a door you're trying to open. All muscle groupings such as these hand-eye coordinations fall under the guidance of the cerebellum.

The largest part of the brain is the cerebrum. It is composed of two cerebral hemispheres, the right and left, which together make up about 70 percent of the entire nervous system. On the surface of the cerebrum is the cerebral cortex, which is covered with a maze of fissures. It is about 3 to 4 millimeters (¼ inch) thick and surrounds both cerebral hemispheres. Like a giant soup kettle, this is the area of the brain where all the sensory input is mixed and blended together to produce our conscious actions. Ideas, emotions, and memory all arise from this area of the brain, as do speech, intelligence, and learning.

The same folds can be found in the same place on all human brains. These creases are like the X's marking the path on treasure maps; they separate specific regions, or lobes, of the cerebral cortex. There are four of these lobes. At the rear is the *occipital lobe*, which unlocks visual treasures like color, size, form, and movement; on the side above the ears is the *temporal lobe*, which maintains the booty of three of the five senses, hearing, sight, and smell; behind the forehead is the *frontal lobe*, which houses reason, emotion, speech, and judgment; and under the scalp is the *parietal lobe*, which oversees its cache, the remaining senses, taste and touch.

Connecting the two hemispheres of the cerebrum is the *corpus callosum*. As we will see when we discuss the two sides of the cerebrum in more detail, the white matter of the corpus callosum is the only bridge between the two hemispheres.

From the largest part of the brain, we now move to the smallest, the *pituitary gland*. If ever there was a case for size having nothing to do with importance, the pituitary would be exhibit number one. This pea-sized gland pro-

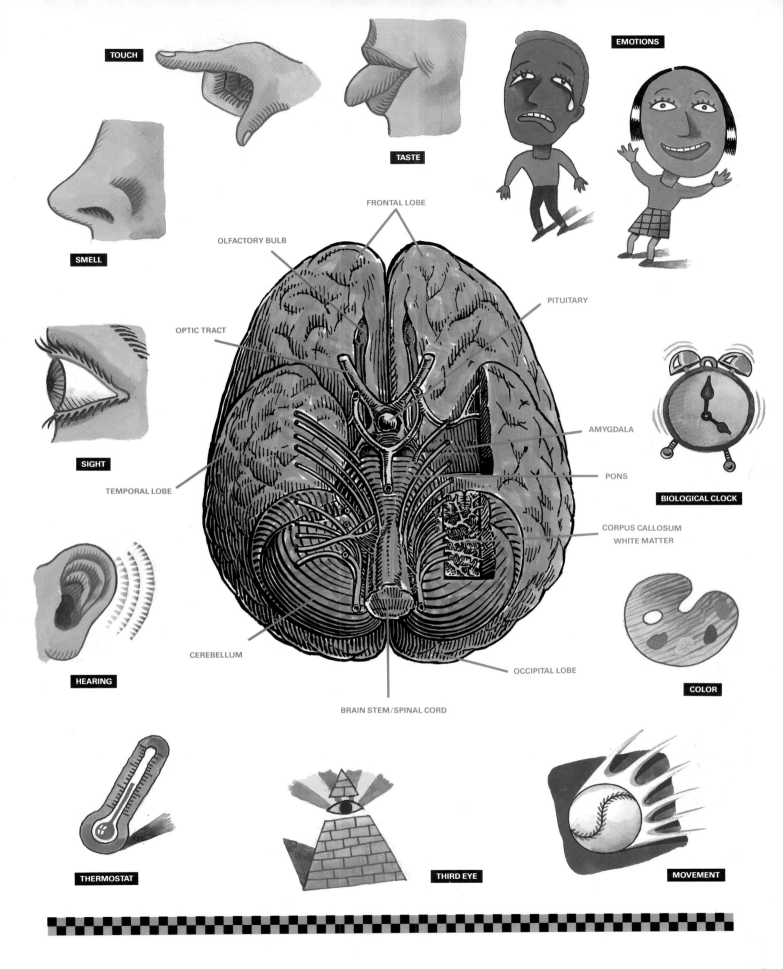

TOUCH

TASTE

EMOTIONS

SMELL

FRONTAL LOBE

OLFACTORY BULB

PITUITARY

OPTIC TRACT

AMYGDALA

SIGHT

PONS

BIOLOGICAL CLOCK

TEMPORAL LOBE

CORPUS CALLOSUM
WHITE MATTER

CEREBELLUM

HEARING

OCCIPITAL LOBE

COLOR

BRAIN STEM/SPINAL CORD

THERMOSTAT

THIRD EYE

MOVEMENT

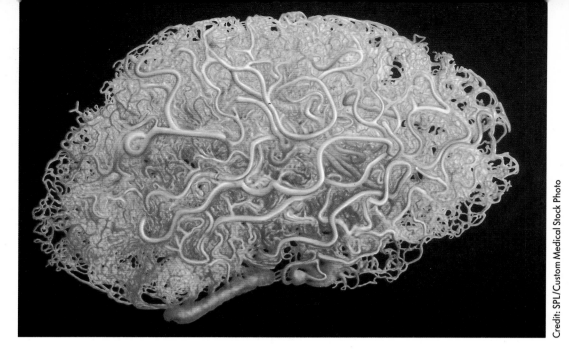

Artist's rendering of the numerous blood vessels servicing the human brain

Credit: SPL/Custom Medical Stock Photo

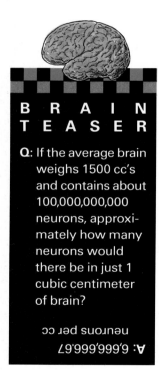

duces the hormones that are actively changing the lives of most young people. The pituitary directs physical growth. Also, it helps children mature sexually. In addition, it sends messages to other organs of the body, like the thyroid, to instruct them how to do their jobs. The pituitary is like a conductor in an orchestra who helps all the instruments play together to make harmonious music.

The pituitary gland has a direct supervisor that lies right above it. This supervisor is known as the *hypothalamus* (hi-po-THAL-a-mus). Located just above the midbrain, the hypothalamus is the body's thermostat: it maintains body temperature. It also influences heart rate, sexual development, and sleep. Dieters should be well aware of the hypothalamus, because it has to do with how the body uses and stores fat. And the hypothalamus also enables us to have emotional expression—to laugh and to cry, for example.

Right next door to the hypothalamus is the *thalamus*. This party of brain cells mixes together impulses from the senses. It is very important as a relay station for impulses that are later coordi-

nated by the cerebral cortex. As we will also see when we talk about how the brain evolved, the thalamus is a leftover of our reptilian/amphibian brain. More on that shortly.

Another tiny structure inside the brain is the *pineal gland*. This reddish-gray, pinecone-shaped lump was once considered to be the mystic "third eye." In fact, there are many people today who believe the pineal gland is the resting place of ancient knowledge and the human soul. But that is a spiritual matter and not a scientific one. Most scientists do agree that this little gland is our inner timekeeper, having a close relationship to light and our biological clock. This inner clock is tied to the Earth's daily rotation around the Sun. With its connection to light, the pineal gland has been compared to the eye's retina. So, maybe the pineal gland is a "third eye." From an evolutionary standpoint, every brain from the beginning of braindom has contained some form of pineal gland.

Did the human brain actually evolve from creatures besides humans or even monkeys? You bet.

THE BRAIN MAZE

Part Fish, Part Frog,

THE EVOLUTION OF THE BRAIN began, like all of life, in water. One fascinating fact about the evolution of the human brain is that as it developed from lower creatures, fish, frogs, and the like, it never got rid of the old bits and pieces.

In order for large-brain creatures like humans to develop, two basic changes had to take place. The first development can be seen in fish, such as the amphioxus, whose nerves have been separated from their gut region. The second change, which is also evident in the amphioxus, was the relocation of the nerves' regulation into a central control station.

Fish were the first creatures on Earth to develop a backbonelike tube to hold all the nerves that traveled to and from the various sense receptors and muscles. It was from this humble start that the spinal cord would later develop. At the head end of these prehistoric tubes, it is believed that three swellings occurred which were associated with special senses: the forebrain (smell), the midbrain (vision), and the hindbrain (balance and stability, or equilibrium). *All* brains that followed simply added onto this arrangement.

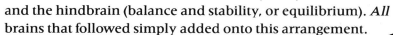

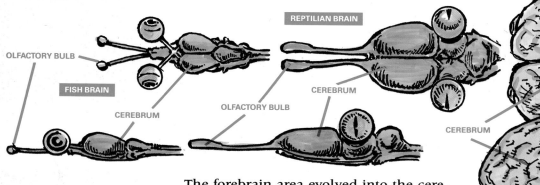

OLFACTORY BULB

FISH BRAIN

CEREBRUM

REPTILIAN BRAIN

OLFACTORY BULB

CEREBRUM

CEREBRUM

HUMAN BRAIN

The forebrain area evolved into the cerebrum; the midbrain, into the visual component called the *optic tectum*; and the hindbrain, into the cerebellum. Among the largest parts of the fish brain are the optical lobes. As with most evolutionary developments, this one is a necessity for survival. If a fish doesn't keep its eyes open to what's happening around it, it quickly becomes someone else's lunch. This optical unfolding was important in human brain development, too, because it eventually formed a thin gray blanket of cells that would become the cortex. Because it covers the surface, the cortex allows a lot more connections between nerves with only a small increase in size. It also means more brain cells can be jammed together in this small space.

Sight isn't the only area that advanced brain development. Smell (or the olfactory sense) was also important. It was from the olfactory region of the early fish brains that the cerebrum area began to evolve. But it was not until amphibians and reptiles began leaving the seas that the cerebrum became the largest part of the brain. For creatures crawling around on land, a sense of smell was more important than the visual needs of beasties swimming around in water.

As brain power began to move from the midbrain region and the large optic septums of fish toward the forebrain and the olfactory lobes of amphibians, the brain

All Human

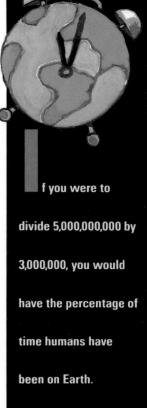

developed the thalamus. The thalamus coordinates sight, smell, and hearing, which are essential ingredients for surviving on land and avoiding the "someone else's lunch" syndrome. In humans, the forward push of the brain also began in the olfactory areas, swelling out and over all of the other areas to eventually form the cerebral hemispheres. With this push, the cerebrum took control from the thalamus and became leader of the brain.

In mammals, there were three steps in the development of the cerebral cortex. The first, concerned primarily with smell, was the growth of the *paleocortex*. On top of the paleocortex, the second layer emerged, which began to mix the different senses. This was called the *archicortex*. The final thrust, which buried the amphibian brain even deeper inside the human brain, was the formation of the *neocortex*. This step forged the archicortex into the *hippocampus*, which, as we will see later, is involved with the storage of memory. And then the neocortex began its evolutionary trek toward the current cerebral cortex.

The neocortex's trip to present-day cerebral top gun is pretty incredible, too. The first humanlike brains belonged to characters known as *Australopithecus africanus*. Their brains were only about 500 cubic centimeters large, or about one-third the size of human brains today. So how, in only 3 million years, did the brain triple in size? Although 3 million years may seem like a long time, on the evolutionary scale, it's a mere drop in the bucket of time. Consider that the Earth itself is about 5 billion years old.

The key to understanding evolution, however, is in the number of generations things have to develop. For the human brain, that's about 12 million generations. Over this period of time, it would be possible for each generation to have a little bit larger brain and be just a tiny bit smarter than the previous one.

If you were to divide 5,000,000,000 by 3,000,000, you would have the percentage of time humans have been on Earth.

Bigger Doesn't Mean Better

SIZE alone is not the issue. The ratio of body size to brain size is.

The human brain weighs about 2½ pounds, which is about 2% of a person's body weight.

The world's largest brain belongs to the sperm whale, weighing in at 20 pounds—0.02% of body weight.

Brain weight to body weight isn't the only factor. The size of the cerebrum in humans distinguishes us from other creatures. Those creatures with less-developed cerebrums or none at all operate much more on automatic pilot than we humans do.

Doing the Synaptic

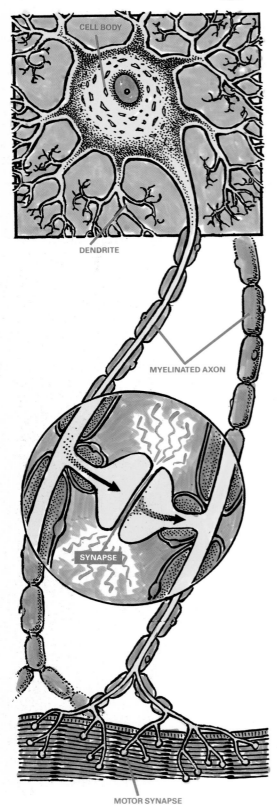

CELL BODY

DENDRITE

MYELINATED AXON

SYNAPSE

MOTOR SYNAPSE

HOW DOES THE BRAIN, and all its different parts, do all the things it is supposed to do? This fundamental question takes us back to the 100 billion neurons, or brain cells, that make up the brain.

Each neuron is a nerve cell made up of four different parts. The first is the *cell body*. This is the command control center of the neuron. It may be star shaped, or it may look like a pyramid or even a pear. Contained inside this cell body is the *nucleus* of the cell, where the DNA, the material responsible for life itself, is stored. Circling around the nucleus is a fluid called the *cytoplasm*, and swimming around the cytoplasm are tiny oval-shaped bits called *mitochondria*, which are the power plants that provide the energy for the cell. When groups of neuron cell bodies get together, they form the gray matter of the brain. When they are spread out into a sheet, they form what is called a cortex.

Surrounding the cell body are numerous little fingerlike branches called *dendrites*. Dendrites connect the neuron to the other neurons surrounding it. In addition to these fingery dendrites, the neuron has a long offshoot called an *axon*. In some cases, as in the connections between the feet and the spinal cord, axons can be almost three feet long. It's down the axon's path that the electrical nerve signals or impulses in the brain are passed. And like an electrical extension cord, the axon is covered with a thin, fatty coating called *myelin*. This coating protects the message traveling down the axon from being confused with other messages in other axons. The myelin also gives the white matter of the brain, which is composed of bundles of axons, its color. For example, the cerebellum, which is covered by a thin gray matter cortex, is mostly white matter, composed of 95 percent axons and 5 percent cell bodies.

As axons separate from the gray matter parts of the brain, they collect into bundles of material called *nerve tracts*. These tracts go from the brain to various parts of the body or to and from the spinal cord. The nerve tract that runs from the brain to the eye, the optic nerve, is made up of over 10 million different axons.

At the bottom of each axon are the *synapses*, which are the points where the brain signals take their great leap from one brain

Leap

cell to the next. The gorge across which these electrical impulses must leap is less than 2 millionths of an inch wide. The brain message takes about 1/1000th of a second to make the leap, which is about 500 times faster than a blink of an eye.

Just before the synaptic gap are microscopic pockets called *vesicles* which contain chemical transmitters. When a message arrives, the vesicle releases its chemical transmitters into the synapse. This release creates a chemical imbalance. Just as when hot air and cold air come together to make the electrical charge known as lightning, these chemical transmitters combine and create an electrical charge. This electrical charge allows the message being transmitted to leap from synapse to synapse, just as you would leap if you received an electrical charge. The synapses, however, are not just phone lines to relay idle brain chats. It is generally believed that the messages transmitted during the synaptic leap help the brain figure out what it knows.

We mentioned earlier that there are about 100 billion neurons in the brain, or about as many stars as in our galaxy. When synapses are mixed in, the number increases tremendously. For example, in monkeys, a single neuron can make up to 10,000 synaptic connections to other neurons. When we multiply that number times the 100 billion neurons contained in the brain, we've got more than 100 trillion connections between synapses. That's more than 200,000 times the number of people on Earth or over 2,000 galaxies worth of stars.

One of the first complete pictures of these neurons and their connections was made by a man named Camillo Golgi. He produced a stain out of silver salts that, for reasons still not clear today, selects only certain brain cells and dyes those cells from cell body and dendrite all the way to synapse. Many consider these beautiful Golgi stains to be the Mona Lisas of scientific portraits.

It's amazing, but these billions of neurons and trillions of connections are all crammed into the small space of the skull. Here they are squished, folded, and blended together to make up the

Getting the Message Across

The fastest neural responses make the trip at 400 feet per second, which is about 360 miles per hour.

Slower responses move about 18 inches per second, or close to one mile per hour.

Distances and speed don't always tell the whole story. A 360-mile-an-hour response may only have to travel one foot, and an 18-inch-per-second response may have to travel less than one inch.

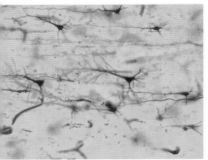

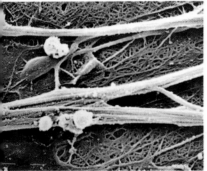

Close-up view of neurones in the cerebral cortex showing central cell bodies, dendrites, and axons

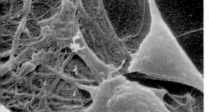

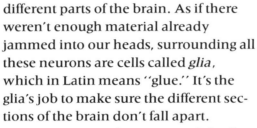

Synapse between two neurones in the cerebral cortex. The synaptic gap appears deep red; the vesicles are the red-yellow spheres above the gap.

different parts of the brain. As if there weren't enough material already jammed into our heads, surrounding all these neurons are cells called *glia*, which in Latin means ''glue.'' It's the glia's job to make sure the different sections of the brain don't fall apart.

Neurons are also very special cells, because unlike other cells in the body, neurons don't produce more neurons. The number of brain cells we're born with is approximately the number we have to use throughout our lives. And that number is constantly shrinking. Brain cells die out on the order of thousands a day. But don't worry, with hundreds of billions of neurons at the

ready, losing a thousand or so a day is not a great loss.

If we were to magnify the clumps of neurons running throughout the brain, we would see that they form a maze of connections. Actually, this tangled web looks more like a bowl of spaghetti than what it is, an organized network of cells delivering information at remarkable speeds. The design of this pasta network allows the brain to take a lot of different routes to come up with the same response. Because of all the alternate brainways available to get a message across, the brain can survive thousands of neurons dying on a daily basis and still continue its work without a problem.

The Brain Team:
The Brain and the Central Nervous System

OW THAT THE MAJOR PLAYERS of the brain have been identified, we can see how these neurons and glia join together to form a team that can produce all the information our bodies need to survive. In the brain, this team is called a system, and in combination with the spinal cord, this system is known as the *central nervous system*. The central nervous system, or CNS, electronically and chemically connects all the ingredients along the body's pathways so that what the right hand is doing is known by the brain and the rest of the body. The basic ingredient of this system is the neuron.

To understand how this system works, we must first talk about the kinds of brain highways, or brainways, that carry CNS messages along. There are basically two kinds of brainways, those that transmit signals out to the body, *efferent* nerves, and those that carry signals back to the brain for processing, *afferent* nerves. These two brainways are further divided into two different thoroughfares. Nerves that travel directly to the sense organs—ears, eyes, nose, tongue, and skin—are called *sensory* nerves. Those leading to the muscles and glands are called *motor* nerves. There is also a special kind of motor nerve that belongs to the autonomic nervous system, which oversees details the brain doesn't have to think about, like breathing, blood circulation, and digestion.

It was once thought that afferent nerves (those that bring information to the brain) are only made up of sensory nerves, and efferent nerves (those that take information out to the body) are only motor nerves, linked to the muscles and glands. But then scientists discovered efferent nerves that are also brainways to the senses.

MOTOR

SENSORY

AUTONOMIC

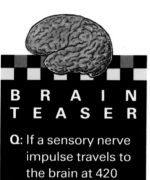

These efferent nerves going to the senses allow us to control our reactions to the information we get from the senses. One example often used is tickling. When we're willing to be tickled, we can't stop laughing. If we don't want to be tickled, we only feel the pressure from someone's touch. This also explains why when we are hurt, a mother's touch feels so much better than anyone else's—because these efferent nerves carry our reaction to the touch.

The brain is the control tower for the incoming and outgoing electrical and chemical nerve transmissions. The brainways are built by connecting the axon of one neuron through the synapse to the dendrite of a neighboring neuron and then to the cell body. The process is repeated again and again, stretching out like a string of blocks with microscopic synaptic gaps between each, sending their message up to the brain. These brainways also leave the brain, move down the spinal cord, and then move out to the different parts of the body.

Picture a light switch on the wall. When the switch is flipped on, it makes an electronic connection that starts electricity flowing down the wire. When the electricity reaches the light bulb, it turns on. This is very similar to what happens in the body. If we were to touch something hot, the touch-sensory afferent nerve, or sense receptor, in our finger would send an electronic message from the finger to the brain, and the brain would light up. The brain would then send an efferent nerve message to the vocal chords, which would send out a scream of pain, and another efferent message to your finger to get it out of the way.

The sensory receptor's job is to translate the information it receives, the burning touch, into a language that the central nervous system understands. Like the electrical switch, which allows electricity to speak to the light, the language of the CNS is the turning on of the axon. The axon then sends the message that it has been turned on to the cell body, which sends the message to the dendrite, which sends the message across its synapse to its neighboring axon, which sends it up to its cell body and eventually up the brainway to the brain.

The sense receptors in the body are very specialized. They can only translate special kinds of information. For example, if we were to shine a light into someone's ear, the ear could not translate that information to the brain. But if we were to speak into someone's ear, that message would arrive in the brain loud and clear. The sense receptor in the ear has only one way to translate a message into brain-talk: it turns its axons on. The only way we can tell the difference between axon messages is by how often the axon is turned on. This is called frequency, or how many times something happens. For example, a whisper turns the axons of the ear on less frequently than rock 'n' roll music would. We'll talk more about these responses when we discuss the different senses.

For now, however, we simply need to understand that the brain and the spinal cord make up a system—the central nervous system. The CNS takes information in, translates it into a language the

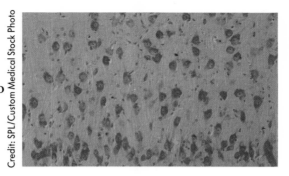

A section of nerve tissue showing groupings of neurones

brain understands, and sends it along the brainways to the brain, which then relays messages back out. The brainways of the system are built from axon to cell body to neighboring axon. The messages traveling along the brainways are electrical and chemical. The system is simple. Even so, no one has ever completely traced a brainway, from axon to axon, because there are so many connections.

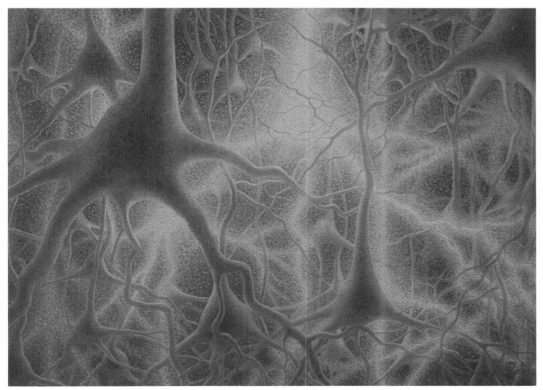

Artist's rendering of a neural network

The Young Brain

F WE'RE BORN with just about all the neurons we're ever going to have in our lives, why can we do so little our first few years? It's true that we come fully equipped with nearly a complete set of neurons at birth. We also come complete with two hands, two feet, two eyes, two ears, a nose, and various other parts that will serve us throughout our lives. But like all the other parts of the body, the brain still has to develop and mature.

Just counting basic parts, all healthy human brains are the same. They're made up of the same bits and pieces, and when body size is accounted for, they all weigh about the same. Somewhere along the line, however, brains start to go their own way. Some people are smarter than others, some are more creative, some are better at math, some are loud, some are not, and some are less of everything. How these differences take place has had scientists, psychologists, and philosophers questioning, guessing, and postulating for thousands of generations.

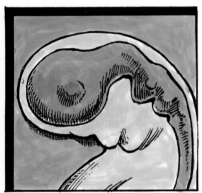

THREE-WEEK EMBRYO

The brain first begins to form when the embryo is about eighteen days old. At the time, the embryo is nothing more than two hollow balls of cells. At the seam where the two balls of cells touch, a hardening takes place, and this edge changes into what is called the neural groove. The brain will form from the head end of this groove, as do the eyes, ears, and nose. Over the next week or so, the groove deepens into a channel and forms the neural tube. This tube will eventually become the spinal cord. Next, the brain develops three swellings, the forebrain, the midbrain, and the hindbrain.

Over the next few months, neurons and glia cells begin their population explosion. To reach the 100 billion neuron level, it is estimated that neuron production must take place at a rate of close to 250,000 neurons a minute. If we divide that by 60, we can find out how many neurons are born each second.

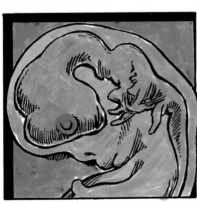

SEVEN-WEEK EMBRYO

As the neural tube begins to develop into the spinal cord, the neurons and glia start to move up to the head end of the tube. About 7 weeks into this process, the three-part brain divides into a five-part brain. The forebrain separates into the thalamic region and the area that will eventually become the cerebral hemispheres.

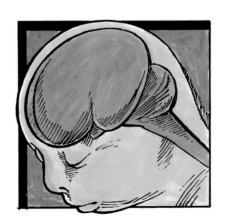

FOUR-MONTH FETUS

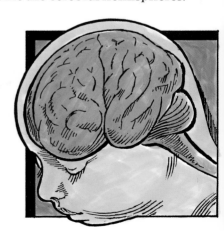

NEWBORN INFANT

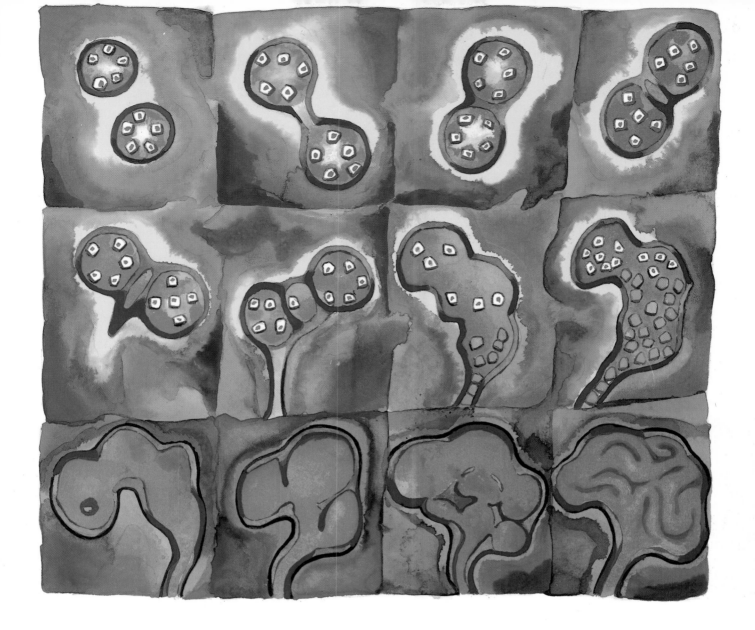

By this time, the cerebral hemispheres are already forming into two bulges. With all this growth, the tube isn't large enough to hold all these pieces, and it develops a couple of kinks, which puts the brain at the proper position in relation to the spinal cord.

Just down from the hindbrain, the cerebellum starts to develop. At the same time, two little cuplike growths begin pushing out from the forebrain. These will become the eyes and the optic nerve.

At the end of three months in the mother's womb, the cerebrum, cerebellum, thalamus, and hypothalamus are visible. By the fifth month, the cerebral cortex is beginning to take on its wrinkled and fissured look. Even with this rapid deployment of brain equipment, when a child is born, the brain is only about one-fourth the size it will be as an adult. In six months, it will be one-half the adult size; at 2 ½ years, three-fourths adult size; and at 10 years old, 95 percent.

If all the neurons are already in

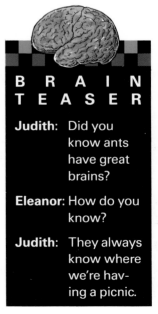

B R A I N
T E A S E R

Judith: Did you know ants have great brains?

Eleanor: How do you know?

Judith: They always know where we're having a picnic.

Glia Cell

As we have said, neurons do not divide or multiply; they also don't add, only subtract. Does that mean we have holes in our brains when these cells die? No. Glia, or glue, cells fill the space left by a departed neuron. Unlike neurons, glia cells can divide and multiply. And when we're born, we have nowhere near the number of glia cells we will as we get older. Eventually, glia cells will make up about half the volume of the brain. With approximately 10 glia cells for each neuron, that makes about one trillion glia cells in a mature brain. Outside of the support they provide the neurons, scientists are not completely sure what other jobs the glia cells may perform.

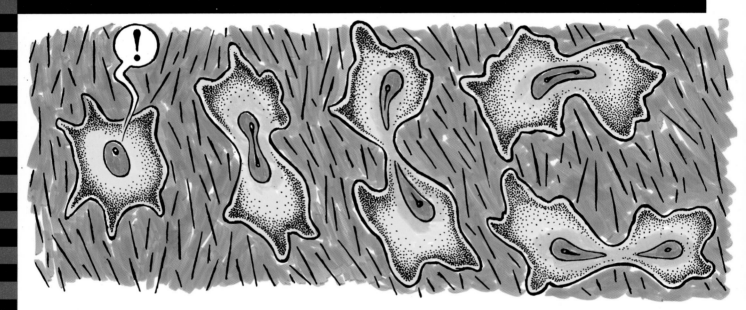

place, what causes the continued growth of the brain? The answer is the continual division of glia cells and the laying down of myelin, the fatty coating that covers the axon like the plastic coating around an electrical cord. When a baby is born, the brain has very little myelin and a lot of exposed axons. The process of wrapping all the brain's billions of axons in myelin will go on until adulthood.

Also, at birth, the cerebral cortex is not as ready for action as the lower brain—the medulla, pons, and thalamus. The first area of the cortex to develop is the part that controls movement of the upper body. This is the motor cortex. Just after a baby is born, the sensory cortex areas begin to develop, followed very quickly by the visual cortex. Scientists think this order is important. The most important action for a newborn baby is the movement of its upper body, touch, taste, smell, and hearing, which are all important with respect to feeding, are next in line. Sight, not essential at birth, follows later.

By the time a baby is three months old, its brain has developed incredibly. Its arms and hands have greater control than when it was born. The baby is actually able to grasp things with its hands—usually a bunch of your hair if you happen to be close. A three-month-old is also capable of focusing its eyes on things and then able to move its hands after those things. It is also able to distinguish voices, especially its mother's, as its hearing develops.

Inside the brain, the neurons' dendrites and axons are growing in length and thickness, and the myelin is beginning to form. As this process continues, by six months, a baby is able to roll over and sit without being propped up. By seven to eight months, the baby is crawling, getting into everything, and trying to put anything available in its mouth. By nine months, the baby is standing, and by a year, it's starting to walk.

All of these events seem to happen around the same time that myelin is covering up the axons controlling these areas. It is still unclear, however, whether the signals being sent along these brainways start the myelin covering process or if the myelin covering process allows the information to travel along the brainway.

From this point on, scientists don't have a lot of information about how the brain develops. We know that we continue to cover axons with myelin through adulthood. And we do know that we can do more and different kinds of things as we grow older. For example, we are able to read, write, and speak much better than a baby, or even a five-year-old. We are able to think of ideas, solve math problems, and be creative in ways we never could when we were younger. All of this is because the brain has continued to develop its brainways, paving them with myelin to carry the heavy traffic of our thoughts, feelings, senses, creative impulses, and body movements.

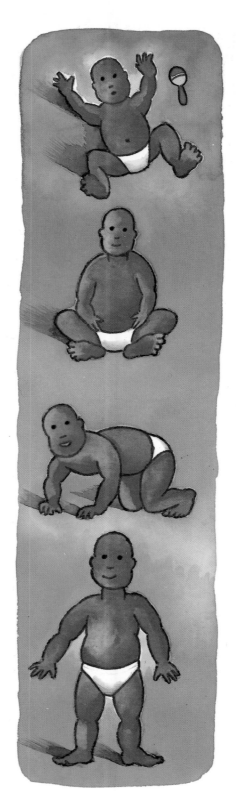

THREE MONTHS

The baby is able to grasp things with its hands

SIX MONTHS

The baby is able to roll over and sit up

EIGHT MONTHS

The baby is crawling

NINE MONTHS

The baby is standing and by a year starting to walk

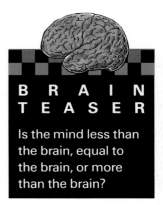

**B R A I N
T E A S E R**

Is the mind less than the brain, equal to the brain, or more than the brain?

On Your Feet—Walking

Y THE TIME MOST CHILDREN are about a year old, they're on their feet, balancing and walking as best they can. As they become more coordinated over the next few years, and the brain-to-muscle connections are better developed, a toddler's walking more closely resembles normal walking.

Humans are the only creatures on Earth who walk on two feet. One of the first human-type walkers was once again our old friend *Australopithecus*. This means manlike creatures have been walking for about 3½ million years (and boy, are they tired).

To make the transition from walking on all fours to walking on two feet, some very complex changes had to take place in the nervous system. We had to have a more well-developed ability to see, hear, and smell and the added ability to be able to change our walking stride at a moment's notice. We also had to have the *desire* to walk upright as well as the genetic ability to do so. We can see this desire in babies who when they see everyone around them walking, struggle to do the same. They try to stand, holding onto anything they can. Then, with constant practice and a lot of falling down and continued desire, they master the ability to walk on two feet.

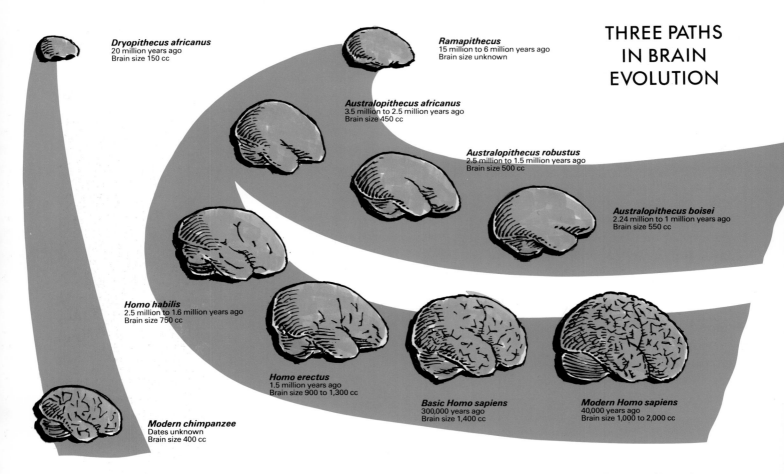

Dryopithecus africanus
20 million years ago
Brain size 150 cc

Ramapithecus
15 million to 6 million years ago
Brain size unknown

THREE PATHS IN BRAIN EVOLUTION

Australopithecus africanus
3.5 million to 2.5 million years ago
Brain size 450 cc

Australopithecus robustus
2.5 million to 1.5 million years ago
Brain size 500 cc

Australopithecus boisei
2.24 million to 1 million years ago
Brain size 550 cc

Homo habilis
2.5 million to 1.6 million years ago
Brain size 750 cc

Homo erectus
1.5 million years ago
Brain size 900 to 1,300 cc

Basic Homo sapiens
300,000 years ago
Brain size 1,400 cc

Modern Homo sapiens
40,000 years ago
Brain size 1,000 to 2,000 cc

Modern chimpanzee
Dates unknown
Brain size 400 cc

Taken from depiction of Leakey's view of evolution of human brain, Encyclopaedia Britannica USA

Upright

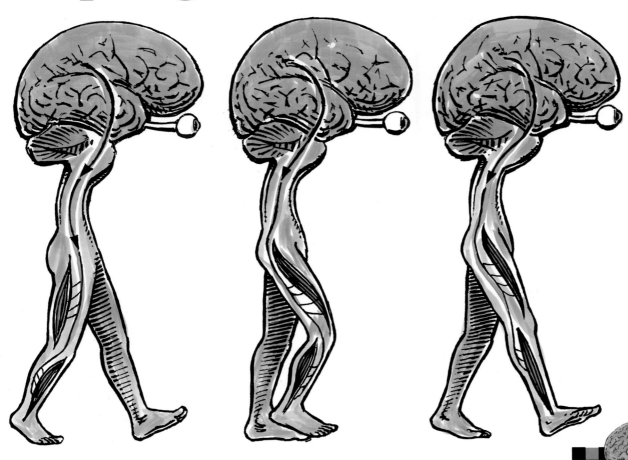

To accommodate the muscle movements for walking, the brain uses the motor areas of the cerebral cortex (the motor cortex) and the cerebellum for balance. The leg muscles are contracted by a series of rhythmic bursts from the motor cortex down the brainways to the legs. There are two main brainways that control walking which run down both sides of the spinal cord. One begins in the motor cortex, the other in the medulla. Since each walking step on two feet requires a contraction of the muscles, the major brainway for walking is the one beginning in the motor cortex. It is also thought that as the foot is traveling down to the ground, it turns on the organs in the inner ear, which further helps with ability to keep our balance. Walking on two feet also requires a great deal of sensory feedback from the legs to the central nervous system.

In all, the machinery necessary to allow humans to walk took over a million years, or over five million generations of humans, to develop. Those first steps forward on two feet were incredibly important to human evolution. Had our ancient ancestors never stepped forward, we would never have freed our hands to develop the use of tools.

Making Sense of the

HE CREAMY TASTE OF CHOCOLATE, the reverberating sounds of rock 'n' roll, the smell of roses on a cool morning, the sight of the endless ocean, the gentle touch of a spring rain—all of these wonderful life events are brought to you by your sensory nerves.

As we mentioned earlier, there are two kinds of brainways, afferent and efferent. Those coming from the sensory receptors are afferent. Those going from the motor cortex in the brain to the muscles are primarily efferent. When a sensory receptor in the foot is triggered by stepping on a tack, the signal travels up the brainways, through the spinal cord, to the cerebral cortex and sensation control central, which is located in the middle of the cortex. If the tack entered the left foot, the message would cross over and be received by the sensation control central on the right side of the brain.

Each of the other senses has its own control tower in the cortex. Sight central is located at the back of the brain just above the cerebellum. Smell central is located above and just in front of the ears, and hearing is located just behind the ears. All the sensory control centers are connected by brainways that also run to the area of the brain that controls our memory, called the *limbic system*.

TOUCH

Our bodies are covered with a layer of skin, which, in turn, is covered from head to toe with sensory receptors. These receptors come in a variety of shapes and sizes. Some are shaped like light bulbs, others like CDs, and still others are cylindrical.

Each shape senses different things—allowing us to feel the difference between a hard tabletop and a soft ball of cotton, a dry towel or a wet one, sandpaper or smooth marble. Skin receptors also sense pressure. The hairs that cover your body are surrounded by sense receptors. If a bug or spider were to walk across your arm, the hair's sensors would be the first to feel the intruder.

From the body's point of view, the most important skin sensors are the pain receptors. These receptors are scattered at various levels through the skin. The reason they are so important is that they warn the body that it is being hurt. There are pain receptors inside your body as well. When they are set off, a chemical release is triggered which starts the electrical relay race up the brainways to the brain. Because the sense control centrals are directly connected to our memory, we

AFFERENT

EFFERENT

Senses

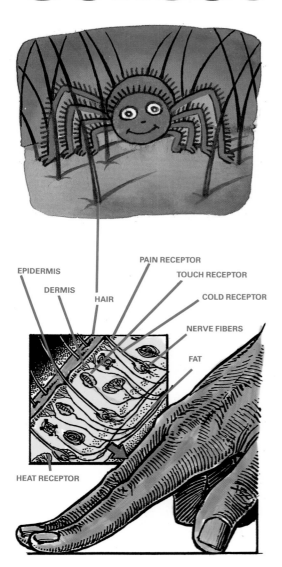

EPIDERMIS
DERMIS
HAIR
PAIN RECEPTOR
TOUCH RECEPTOR
COLD RECEPTOR
NERVE FIBERS
FAT
HEAT RECEPTOR

often react to pain we have experienced before by automatically shortcutting the normal circuitry to the brain. This is called a reflex action.

The body also feels pleasurable sensations. The warmth of the Sun on a winter day, a refreshing dunk in a pool in summer, the reassuring stroke of a parent's hand when we're sad. All these sensations are received by the touch sensors and are relayed to the brain, where they are instantaneously sorted and appropriate responses sent back to the muscles.

TASTE

The sensory receptors for taste, taste buds, cover your tongue. A full-grown adult has about 9,000 of these tasters; a baby has even more. Whereas an adult's taste buds are primarily on the tongue (some are at the back of the throat and on the roof of the mouth), a baby's taste buds are layered throughout its mouth. Taste buds are called ''buds'' because they resemble the bud of a flower. They are filled with receptor cells that have tiny hairs.

When we bite into a piece of food, we chew it first, mixing it with the liquid in our mouths, saliva. As we do this, the food and saliva bathe the surface of the tongue, and the taste buds get their first taste of what we're eating. The small hairs on the buds pick up the liquid, and the receptor cells tell the nerves in the tongue what they think of the taste. The nerves then transmit that message up to the brain. If the taste is good, the brain sends an efferent message down to the vocal cords, and we say, ''Mmmmmm.'' If the taste is bad, the brain sends the message to the mouth to spit the food out, and we say ''Blech!''

There are four types of taste buds, responding to sweet, sour, bitter, and salt. The sweetness receptors are right up on the front of the tongue, the sour buds are at the back of the tongue, the bitter buds are on the sides, and the salt buds are just to the sides of sweet.

◇ BITTER
△ SWEET
○ SOUR
□ SALT
NERVE FIBERS
SENSORY CELL

**B R A I N
T E A S E R**

Harvey: Why does your brother always go cluck, cluck?

Bill: Because he thinks he's a chicken.

Harvey: Why don't you tell him he's not a chicken?

Bill: Because we need the eggs.

The importance of taste is first and foremost protection. Plants that taste very bitter are often poisonous. Rotten food, which tastes awful, can also cause illness. Being able to tell if something is salty or not is especially important when it comes to drinking, as drinking a lot of salty water would make us sick. And the sweet buds are there to make life wonderful. Some things just work out right.

SMELL

When our amphibian ancestors first crawled out of the oceans onto land, the sense of smell became a primary sense. And there were a lot of smells to smell—approximately 10,000 different ones. The amphibian brain, in fact, developed from the olfactory area of the frontal lobe. There are about 15,000 olfactory nerves at the top of the nasal cavity behind the nose. Jammed into this same small space are about 5 million smell receptors. Each of these receptors responds to only one kind of smell. The combination of these different receptors allows us to tell the difference between those thousands of different aromas.

The nasal receptors pick up smells from the air we breathe in. As with food and saliva that pass across the tongue, air contains particles that cross the receptors at the back of the nose. Tiny hairs pick up the smell from these particles. The hairs transfer the smell impulse to the olfactory nerves, which send it up to the brain for processing and memory response.

As with taste, smell is primarily a warning sense. If something smells bad, like rotten food or spoiled water, the brain sends down an efferent response to the muscles that makes us pull away. Smells that are good, of course, can draw us near. There are plants, like Venus's-flytrap, that in fact use a sweet smell to attract various insects and then

NERVE FIBERS

SINUS CAVITIES

capture them. This is pretty tricky, because most pleasant-smelling things are not dangerous.

Smell and taste are closely linked. Taste is a delicate sense, but when combined with smell, the taste of food can be recognized more easily. This also explains why when we have colds and our noses are plugged up, we lose a great deal of our tasting ability.

You can test this for yourself. Take a piece of fruit and close your eyes. With one hand, hold your nose closed. With the other, take a bite of the piece of fruit. After that take another bite without holding your nose. Which taste was more pronounced?

HEARING

Until now, all the senses we have spoken about have had to do with things we can feel coming in contact with our sense organs. Sound is not like a physical touch, or food on taste buds, or particles in the air we breathe which cross the smell receptors. Sounds are waves, vibrations, which enter the ear and are then transmitted to the brain.

The ear is made up of three parts: the outer ear, the middle ear, and the inner ear. The outer ear directs sounds down a short tube called the *ear canal*. The outer ear and the middle ear are separated by the *eardrum*, which is a thin piece of skin stretched across the end of the ear canal. When sound waves hit the eardrum, it vibrates just like the head on a drum.

These vibrations are sent into the middle ear, where there are three tiny bones called the *hammer*, the *anvil*, and the *stirrup*. These names correspond to the shape of the bones. At the base of the stirrup bone is a piece called the *foot-plate*. This fits up against the inner ear. When a sound is received, the vibrations travel through the hammer, anvil, and stirrup to the footplate. These bones act like a battering ram, pushing the footplate against the inner ear with a force 22 times stronger than the vibration on the outside of the eardrum.

Inside the inner ear is a small space that contains the *cochlea*, which looks like a snail shell. It's actually a tightly coiled tube filled with liquid. The battering from the footplate makes this liquid vibrate and move, and the tiny hairs that line the cochlea pick up this activity. These hairs are attached to millions of sensory cells, which convert the sounds into a coded electrical impulse that the neurons contained in the *auditory nerve* understand. The auditory nerve then transmits this message to the audi-

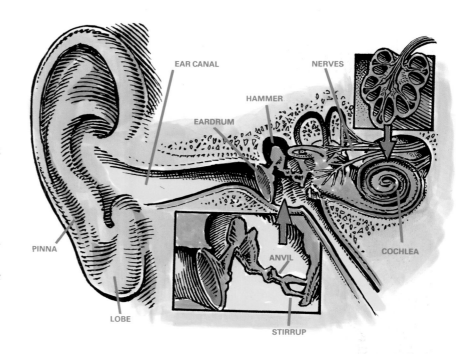

tory part of the cerebral cortex. If the sound received is musical, the auditory cortex sends a message down the motor brainway to the foot, which starts to tap to the rhythm of the music. If the sound is a lion's roar, the motor cortex again sends a message down to the feet, this time to run as fast as they can.

SIGHT

The expression, "A picture is worth a thousand words," points up how important seeing is to all of us. The images that enter our eyes tell us about the world around us. We can know more from one visual picture than from pages of descriptions.

As with the other senses, the brain controls how we see the world. The eye itself is made up of the *cornea*, a clear protective layer on the outside of the eye, the *iris*, the colored portion of the eye that opens and closes the *pupil*, the dark inner hole of the eye through which light passes. The iris, like an automatic camera, decides exactly how much light needs to pass through the pupil so that we can see. At night, the iris expands the pupil to its full opening,

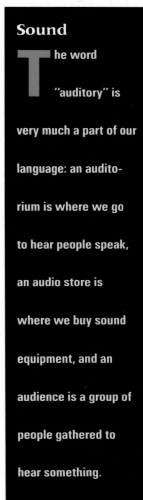

Sound

The word "auditory" is very much a part of our language: an auditorium is where we go to hear people speak, an audio store is where we buy sound equipment, and an audience is a group of people gathered to hear something.

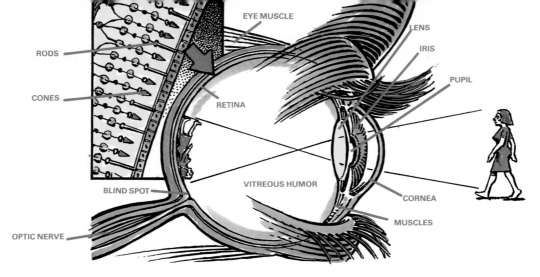

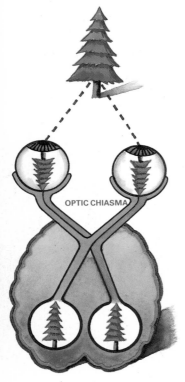

or aperture. In bright sunlight, the iris narrows the opening of the pupil to keep light out.

Once the light travels through the pupil, it goes through the *lens* of the eye. The lens focuses the picture onto the *retina*, which is located at the back of the eye. The retina is the brain's partner in the eye. It contains all the sensory receptors that translate the pictures it sees into the language the brain can understand. The retina is made up of about 6 million sensors called *cones*. Cones allow us to see in bright light and detect all the remarkable colors around us. The retina also has about 120 million other sensors called *rods*. Rods record pictures in black and white; they help us see at night and in very low light.

When the retina sees something, the receptors send the message along the optic nerve to the optic cortex. The picture it sends the brain, like that taken by a camera, is actually upside down. The first synapse it encounters is a group of neuron bodies, gray matter, called the *lateral geniculate body* (referred to as the LGB, to make things a little simpler). By the time the image has reached the LGB, the crossover from right eye to left hemisphere and left eye to right hemisphere has already taken place. The LGB also starts figuring out what the picture is it has received.

It would seem that to have two eyes sending basically the same upside down image to the brain would make things pretty confusing. Especially when each eye is sending its upside down picture to the opposite side of the brain. But there is a method to this madness. By crossing over in this manner, the brain is able to join these two pictures into one image.

Once inside the visual cortex, the brain really starts figuring out what it's looking at. Both the visual cortex on the right side of the brain and the visual cortex on the left side of the brain re-create the pattern received by the two retinas. Then the cortex divides the task of reading this picture. Some neurons respond to the shape of the picture, some respond to its brightness, some determine if it is moving or not. There are also neurons receiving information from the memory storage areas of the brain to see if this image has been seen before. And there are neurons responsible for turning the picture right side up. All of this happens in the twinkling of an eye.

Being able to see is really quite complex. It is so complex, in fact, that it has even led some scientists to think that the brain evolved because it needed to understand all the information the eye was picking up. Whether or not this theory will ever be proven is hard to say. But it is probably safe to say that one picture is worth millions of optic neurons.

Remember When?

HERE ARE SO MANY THINGS to remember—street addresses, phone numbers, names, math problems, batting averages, how to spell, the top ten tunes on the charts, birthdays, people to like, people to avoid, people to love. How does the brain keep track of all these things?

Besides keeping the body alive, memory is one the most important and perplexing responsibilities of the brain. Like Lewis Carroll's description of Alice's passage through the looking glass, the brain is "a wonderland where everything is so strange and uncommon." Memory is a storehouse of experiences we have known. But it does not have to do just with things that happened in the past. Memory is involved in almost everything we do, from relationships with other people to making simple movements when swinging a tennis racket to being able to find our way home.

Memory is affected by all the things we find interesting and by what we believe about the world. It is also influenced by whatever we are involved in at the moment. If we were reading a book, the lives of the characters would be something our memories would store. And it is affected by the mood we are in. If we're in a bad mood, we may remember only bad events; if we're in a good mood, we would probably remember happier events.

As mentioned earlier, memory is closely connected to the temporal lobe of the brain, in an area called the *limbic system*. This is an ancient part of the brain, sometimes referred to as the "animal brain," and it is involved with emotional and instinctive responses. The limbic system is buried beneath the cortex of the brain and is made up of a number of different organs including the *hippocampus* and the *amygdala*. This area is directly connected to the hypothalamus.

The hippocampus is named after its "S"-like shape, which reminded early brain scientists of a sea horse, which is what hippocampus means in Greek. There are two hippocampus organs, one on each side of the brain. In addition to their connection to the hypothalamus, the hippocampus and the entire limbic system are directly connected via brainways to all the senses. This explains why the senses can trigger memories so easily. A particular smell in a grandparent's house

HIPPOCAMPUS

AMYGDALA

LIMBIC SYSTEM

Short-term memory only lasts about a minute and is very limited in content. Any list containing more than seven items should be written down, especially if you're being sent to the store.

Long-term memory can last a lifetime. Just ask a grandparent about his or her childhood.

The information storage capacity of an average brain could fill a 40,000-volume library. But that doesn't mean it would be interesting reading.

can bring back a flood of memories of past Christmas or Thanksgiving holidays.

While the hippocampus is responsible for storing memories that have to do with events, its partner in the limbic system, the amygdala, is responsible for storing memories that have to do with emotions. Therefore, the content of the memory has a great deal to do with where it is finally stored.

Accessing the emotional memories in the amygdala is often more difficult than recalling memories of events stored in the hippocampus. Although some people can recall emotional memories more easily than others.

Memories are recorded in the limbic system with the help of the hypothalamus. The hypothalamus releases a chemical that is transported along the brainways to the limbic system. It is believed that this chemical, *vasopressin*, is directly involved in the recording of memories by the cells of the hippocampus and amygdala. Scientists discovered the role of vasopressin while trying to find out about memory loss. They found that patients who had lost a part of their memory did not have as much of this chemical as those with healthy memories.

There are two basic explanations for why we experience memory loss: one is that the synapse connection of a memory is still present but we are unable to recontact it. The second idea is that we forget because the synapse connection has simply been broken.

In one recent theory of memory, Donald Hebb speculated that as the brain is developing, our experiences form a combination of neurons he calls "brain cell assemblies." Like a series of Lego blocks, there are cell assemblies linked to each of the senses, to particular words, objects, and experiences. These millions of assemblies eventually weave themselves together into a complex Lego construction of all our different sense and experience memories. Forgetting is then a breakdown of the connections between these brain cell assemblies.

There are some people who claim to have forgotten more than most people know. Whether or not this is the case, the human brain can retain an amazing amount of information. But memory isn't something we just have; we can also improve memory with exercises. These exercises are based on forming a mental visual image that reminds us of what we want to remember.

Try this. Go into the kitchen and look around the room. Look carefully at all the different objects—pots, pans, spices, plates, foodstuffs. Identify those objects with something you might be able to visualize—a sugar bowl with a breakfast cereal, a coffee pot with the smell of brewing coffee. Do this for as many objects as you can, and then leave the room. Take a piece of paper and draw a picture of the kitchen, trying to recall as many images and details as you can. Practice this a number of times in different rooms of your house. Can you remember more with each try?

Say That Again

THE WORLD WOULD CER-TAINLY be a different place if somewhere along the line the brain hadn't figured out that it could form sounds and turn those sounds into the communication we call speech. We have not been successful in figuring out how speech evolved. But we do know where in the brain speech is centered.

As we already know, the cerebral cortex is divided into two hemispheres. The left hemisphere is the home of the speech area, now referred to as Broca's area. Paul Broca was a nineteenth-century French scientist who performed an autopsy on a patient who had suffered from aphasia, a disease that would not allow the person to recall certain words. Broca discovered when he sliced into the person's brain that there was a great deal of damage to a particular area in the left hemisphere of the cerebral cortex. Through further experimentation, Broca was able to confirm that this was the speech center.

In the 1950s, Wilder Penfield, a Canadian brain surgeon, continued Broca's work, mapping a series of locations in the left side of the cortex that controlled speech. These included the area that controlled vocalization and the movement of the lips, the jaw, the tongue, and the throat.

Noam Chomsky, a professor of linguistics at the Massachusetts Institute of Technology, has theorized that all human speech at its very roots, regardless of language differences, is identical.

What this means is that in humans, language has been hard wired into the brain, in much the same way that birds are prewired to sing. According to Chomsky, humans must and will speak. It has been shown, however, that when a child has been raised in isolation from other people, he or she doesn't develop the ability necessary for speech.

Whether speech in humans is a foregone conclusion or something learned by accident and passed on from generation to generation, the brain can make lists of different lengths. And much like a computer program produces computer languages, these lists can act on each other in such a way as to produce a human language. Unfortunately, scientists have yet to understand how the brain translates those lists into speech.

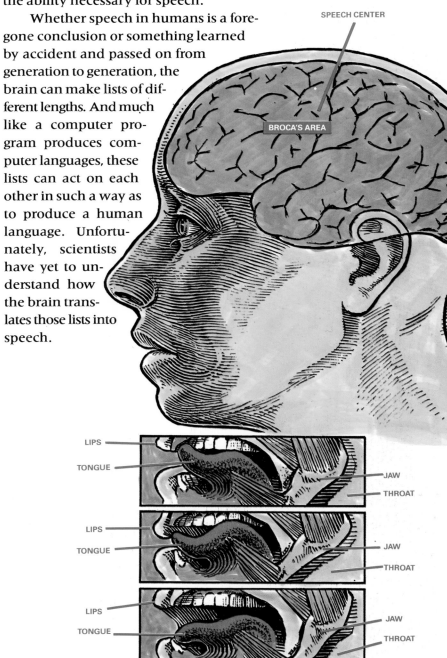

SPEECH CENTER

BROCA'S AREA

LIPS
TONGUE
JAW
THROAT

LIPS
TONGUE
JAW
THROAT

LIPS
TONGUE
JAW
THROAT

29

Thinkers and Feelers,

"**D**IDN'T YOU THINK ABOUT THAT BEFORE YOU DID IT?**"** comes the cry from your parents. Suddenly, you experience a rush of feelings. You feel embarrassed, or you feel sad. In a flash of inspiration, a thought comes to you which provides the solution to the problem. It becomes very clear exactly what details need to be seen to in order to calm your parents. To accomplish this range of actions, the cerebral cortex has become a beehive of activity. Messages are darting across brainways, feverishly moving back and forth between the right and left hemispheres of the brain.

Each hemisphere of the cerebrum has certain responsibilities. The left side of the brain deals more with thinking, reasoning, and speech. It puts things in logical sequence, organizes, and recognizes details. The right brain is more involved with controlling motor skills and movement, fantasies, feelings, and intuition. Intuition is our ability to know something without necessarily having all the facts. Flashes of inspiration, knowing something is going to happen before it happens, knowing something is not quite right without knowing exactly why—these are all examples of intuition. We'll talk more about this later.

The brainway connecting the two sides of the cerebral cortex is the corpus callosum. This white matter mass of axons is the bridge across which messages from the right brain travel over to the left brain to be verbalized. Messages from the left brain also travel over to the right brain whenever a larger picture of an issue is needed.

Roger Sperry and Michael Gazzaniga first realized the difference between the right brain and the left

Intuiters and Sensers

brain in the 1960s. They were working with some patients who had severe epilepsy, a serious disturbance of the brain's electrical patterns. In this case, neurons short circuit and randomly set off messages that can cause a person to pass out. At the same time, these neuron messages are sent out to the muscles, causing uncontrollable movements called convulsions or seizures. A surgical procedure can be performed on people who have life-threatening seizures. In this operation, the corpus callosum is cut, separating the two hemispheres of the cortex.

In 1967, Sperry and Gazzaniga followed up these surgical procedures, studying nine people whose corpus callosum had been cut. They found that by covering the left eye of one of these people and testing each hemisphere of the brain individually, the right side of the brain picked up different information than the left. The left verbally identified things it was able to see. The right could point to and touch objects, but the verbal responses from this side of the brain were usually emotional and unorganized. Sperry's studies of abnormal brains unlocked a treasure chest of experiments and new ideas about the way the brain functions normally—when both sides of the brain work together.

Psychologists have thought for years that there were four basic ways the human brain responded to the world: (1) through its ability to think, (2) through feelings and emotions, (3) through sensations or by way of the senses, and (4) by using intuition.

Credit: SPL/Custom Medical Stock Photo

Using your imagination, what side of the brain would people in these occupations probably use most?

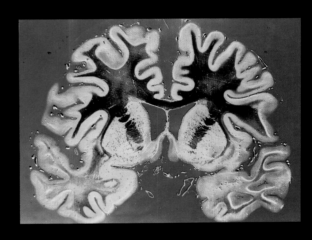

Composer   Businessperson

Physicist   Rock 'n' roll singer

Football player   Engineer

Writer   Architect

Mathematician   Teacher

Sensation tells us simply that something is. This thing exists. We can sense it, but that's all we can do. Thinking tells us *what* that something is. It gives that thing a name. Feelings tell us what that thing means to us, what it's worth to us. Intuition is a little harder to describe, because it has to do with time. Time is hard to touch, but it exists. Things have a past and a future. We can't always see where they come from, and we don't always know where they are going. Being able to know about something outside of its present time is intuition. It's like being able to see the whole picture of something. We often refer to intuition as a hunch.

As humans, we use all these ways to respond to the world. Some people are better at thinking, some are better at recognizing their feelings, some are more aware of their senses, some are more intuitive. Each of these people, however, still uses the other three ways at different times. We can tell which hemisphere of the brain a person uses most by the way he or she is most comfortable responding. Feelers and intuiters are right brain dominant; thinkers and sensation types are more left brain dominant. There's no good or bad, right or wrong, to this division. It is simply the way in which people view the world around them.

The right brain/left brain split also explains events like brainstorms—sudden flashes of inspiration that usually have to do with solving a problem. Basically, brainstorms are a product of intuition; an idea or a thought suddenly becomes crystal clear in our minds. What is hap-

pening inside the brain is that a strong, whole-picture message is being rushed from neuron to neuron across the corpus callosum from the right brain to the left. It arrives suddenly, and unexpectedly, and we can just as suddenly speak about it. Before the storm, we probably had no idea how to describe the solution to the problem.

We might think of insights as similar to brainstorms, also as products of our intuition. It is important to understand that intuition doesn't just appear in the brain out of thin air. It is a combination of what we know, our memories, and our experience that allows us to have intuitive flashes. Insights might be considered as more personal in nature or as having to do with gaining a complete picture of a concept rather than finding a solution to a specific problem.

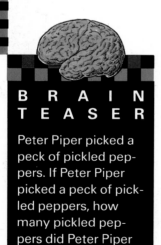

BRAIN TEASER

Peter Piper picked a peck of pickled peppers. If Peter Piper picked a peck of pickled peppers, how many pickled peppers did Peter Piper pick?

A: Eight quarts.

CAT SCANS, PETs, AND MRIs

CAT scans, PETs, and MRIs may sound like a bizarre menagerie, but they are actually three of the newest techniques for taking pictures inside the body.

A CAT scan is a device that measures X rays going through the body from a lot of different directions. "CAT" stands for computerized axial tomography. Using the measurements from these CAT scan X rays, a computer reconstructs whatever part of the body it has been trained on. It is as if the CAT scan takes a series of thin slices of the tissues it is examining and then pieces them back together into a whole, allowing scientists and doctors to examine the tissues of each cut made, without ever having to lift a scalpel.

A PET scan is actually a positive emission tomography. It performs its magic on the subatomic level, by injecting a special substance into the area to be scanned. This material creates positrons, which are particles of antimatter. The antimatter is immediately set upon by its opposite matter, electrons, which neutralize the positrons. In neutralizing these positrons, however, the substance lets off radiation. Detectors can be placed around the body to pick up the radiation being released, 1/15th that of an X ray. The pictures obtained by the path of radiation left by the substance allows scientists and doctors to see hot spots and cold spots in the brain where problems might be encountered.

MRI stands for magnetic resonance imaging. In this process, a person lies inside a giant tube, and radio waves are beamed through the body from different angles. At the same time, the patient is being surrounded by a powerful magnetic field. Different parts of the body absorb radio waves at different frequencies when subjected to a magnetic field. This is something like tuning a radio to different numbers on the dial to get different stations. "We are coming to you live from KBRN, radio brain." Only in this case, the way these different areas absorb the frequencies is measured and then fed into a computer. From this data, the computer reconstructs an image of the internal body showing every nook, cranny, vessel, and nerve.

Credit: Custom Medical Stock Photo

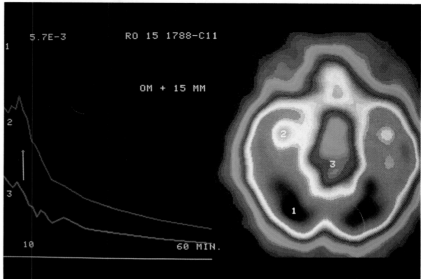

Credit: Custom Medical Stock Photo

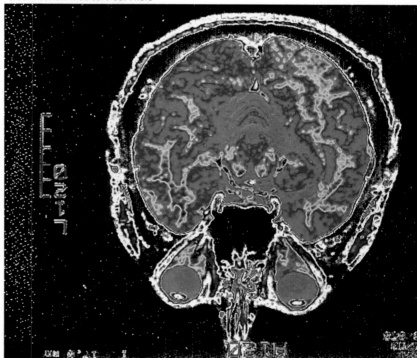

Top photo: PET scan of the brain of a person who suffers from epilepsy
Bottom photo: MRI scan of human brain at eye level

The Amazing World of

BEETHOVEN, BERNSTEIN, and the Beatles wrote music that moved humanity. Rembrandt and Picasso painted remarkable pictures. Shakespeare and Twain wrote inspiring works. Einstein and Newton figured out principles that govern the universe. From what spring of imagination did these creative activities arise? The drive to create art and to creatively solve complex problems of human nature are two remarkable qualities of being human. We are the only living beings on Earth who can imagine something other than what we see before us. No other creature on Earth exhibits this wondrous, often frustrating, ability. And what is even more amazing, we are *all* capable of being creative; we all have in our brains a creative center.

The creative areas of the brain are located in the prefrontal lobes of the right hemisphere of the brain. As we discussed in the right brain/left brain section, the two halves of the cerebral cortex are joined by a mass of white matter axons called the corpus callosum. This is the bridge of synapses between the left hemisphere and its spoken language and speech center and the right hemisphere and its languages of creativity—music, painting, unspoken word images.

Even though the breeding ground of creativity is located in the right hemisphere of the cerebral cortex, it takes the cooperation of both sides to make a creative thought come to life. Crossing that synaptic bridge from the right to the left, to give the unspoken a voice, is a matter of first being receptive to the pictures and sounds that come from the non-vocal right brain.

This crossing usually happens when we are not being overloaded with sensory impulses. This is why creative thoughts often arise in quiet moments. (Although it's probably safe to say that many creative ideas have made themselves known while the senses were being bombarded in a shower.) This random arrival of creative ideas, however, fits with the theory that creativity is somehow connected to the notion of serendipity, finding something without actually looking for it.

It has also been suggested that creativity has a great deal to do with being exposed to other creative ideas. Creativity breeds creativity. Great writers write great books because they have read other great writers. Great painters create great paintings because they have looked at great paintings. Great mathematicians figure out solutions to difficult problems because they have studied other solutions. Great philosophers have realized profound thoughts because they have been exposed to the ideas of other great philosophers.

CORPUS CALLOSUM

OLFACTORY BULB

CEREBELLUM

BRAIN STEM

Creativity

Creativity has nothing to do with greatness, however. Every human is capable of being creative. It has to do with being willing to listen to a part of the brain that is speaking in a quieter and less obvious language. In every brain, there are millions of synapses ready to transmit those imaginative brain pictures across the bridge to the conscious portion of the brain. Having those creative thoughts reach the light of day has a lot to do with keeping the logical/critical functions of the brain from getting in the way when creative ideas come through. Making these creative thoughts real then requires an interplay among all the functions of the brain.

As we will see when we talk about dreams, the impulses of creativity are often fragile, easily squashed by the logical/critical abilities of the brain. Dreams often are remembered because these portions of the brain are at rest and are not filtering out dream images. Since the seeds of creativity have to travel through the kingdom of logic while it is awake, we often have to let down our logical guard for them to come out.

THOSE BIZARRE BRAIN MOVIES

The Man with Two Brains - Steve Martin falls in love with a female brain in a jar.

Donovan's Brain - Scientist is overtaken by a dead man's brain kept alive in his lab.

The Incredible Two-headed Transplant - A schizophrenic monster goes berserk.

X-The Man with X-ray Eyes - the man who could see too much.

The Brain of Blood - A Middle Eastern ruler's brain is transplanted into a monster's body.

The Brain Eaters - Brain eaters from inner earth attach themselves to people's brains.

The Brain from Planet Arous - An evil brain from outer space takes over a scientist.

The Brain Machine - A mind-shattering machine makes people crazy.

The Brain that Wouldn't Die - A mad scientist tries to find a body for his girl friend's decapitated head.

Brainiac - A 300-year-old ghoul eats nothing but brains.

Brainsnatchers - A scientist creates a brain transference machine and goes bonkers trying to transfer his brain into his young lab assistant's.

Brainstorm - A sensory experience device takes the brain to new highs.

Brain Damage - A psychedelic monster goes bananas.

Brain Waves - A female receives the brain of a murdered girl and is then chased by the girl's murderer.

The Man with the Synthetic Brain - A mad scientist creates a man with an electronic brain.

The Man without a Body - Prophet Nostradamus's brain is transplanted into a British man's head.

Dreamland

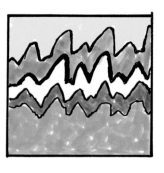

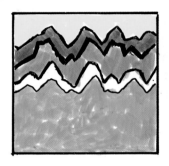

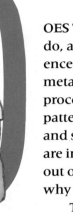

DOES THE BRAIN sleep when we do? Parts of it do, and parts of it do not. By using an electro-encephalograph, also called an EEG, we can attach metal detectors to the skin of the head (a painless procedure) and measure the different electrical patterns of the brain. These patterns vary in size and shape according to the activity in which we are involved. When these patterns are stretched out on an EEG tape, they look like waves, which is why they are commonly known as *brain waves*.

There are four kinds of brain waves: *alpha*, which appear when we are relaxed and awake (these would not be good surfing waves, since their pattern is fast and short); *beta*, which signal deep thinking or motion and have sharp jagged peaks; *delta*, which are the waves of sleep (these would be great surfing waves, as they're slow-moving and large); and *theta*, which are seen during sleep and in the EEGs of babies. Brain waves are only an indication of the activity taking place in the brain. They are not an exact map.

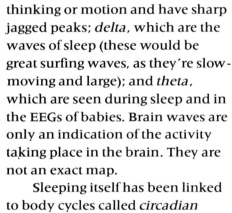

Sleeping itself has been linked to body cycles called *circadian rhythms*. These cycles relate to our inner 24-hour clocks. In some experiments, it has been shown that the thalamus, together with the pineal gland, is responsible for releasing certain chemicals and brain transmitters at different times of the day and night. This periodic release also explains why there are different levels of sleep.

During sleep, we brain surf through five different phases. Stage 1 takes place as we are falling asleep. We glide gently along the wave pattern as we slip in and out of sleep. Our heartbeat and breathing slow down, and our muscles start to relax. Stage 2 is a steep spiral down into sleep. Then we drop off again into Stage 3 and the large

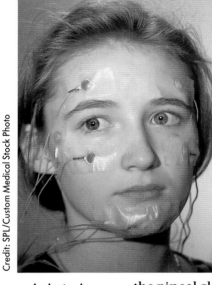

In sleep research electrodes are positioned on the head and neck of the subject and connected to a polysomnograph, a hybrid instrument of an electrocardio-graph (ECG), an electro-encephalograph (EEG), and an electromyograph (EMG). Print-outs provide sleep activity from the heart (ECG) and brain (EEG) and muscle activity in the face and neck.

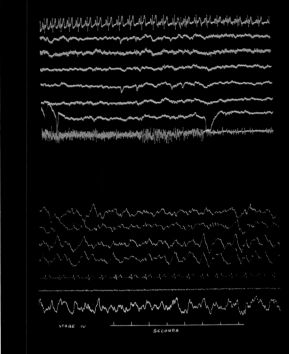

Credit: SPL/Custom Medical Stock Photo

A series of false-color traces showing brain and muscle activity during stage 4 near-REM sleep. Numbering the traces from top to bottom: 1 and 2 show brain activity; 3 shows movement in the right eye; 4 shows movement in the left eye; 5 shows heart activity.

A polysomnogram printout from a subject who is awake, showing traces relating to electrical activity in the brain, heart, and facial muscles.

Credit: SPL/Custom Medical Stock Photo

slow waves of delta sleep. The heartbeat and breathing slow more, body temperature drops, and muscles become even more relaxed. About a half hour after falling asleep, we descend to the final stage (4) of deep sleep. This 30- to 40-minute rhythm of sleep then turns around, and we move back up through the stages to stage 1, though we do not awaken. At this point in the cycle, the eyes begin to flicker, the heartbeat is no longer slow and quiet, and we are in that stage (5) of sleep called REM, which stands for rapid eye movement. This is the time when we are likeliest to be dreaming.

Even though we may be asleep, the brain is anything but quiet. In some cases, the neurons of the brain are busier during sleep than when we're awake. This is obviously happening when we are dreaming.

In spite of all we know about the way the brain works, little is known about dreaming. Scientists believe dreaming is composed of unexpected sensory information that triggers memory patterns. These memories come at a time when the guards and controls of the waking mind have gone off-duty. So rather than halting the progress of these random patterns, they begin to replay. The lack of conscious controls on this event allows for all kinds of blocked information to come out.

Psychologists are of the firm belief that because these dreams are unfiltered, they have important messages for our waking selves. Figuring out what these messages are takes a good deal of training and understanding. One way to think of dreams might be that the brain system is actively trying to resolve problems within itself.

Whatever the reasons for dreaming, one thing is certain, it is a normal part of sleep, and sleep is a normal part of life. We spend about a third of our lives doing it, and if we tried to go without it, we would most certainly die.

Maladies of the

WE ALL, AT ONE TIME or another, have strange thoughts, like a sudden craving for a marshmallow and onion sandwich or wondering how somebody would look without hair. This is normal. We feel sad or disappointed when things don't happen as we'd like. This is normal, too. Or, on occasion, we do funny or crazy things, like running barefoot through the snow or feeling angry for no apparent reason. We have secret thoughts, thoughts we don't really want to share with anyone. All of this is normal behavior, coming from a normal, properly functioning brain.

There are times, however, when the workings of the brain go wrong. Like physical illnesses in the body, there are also illnesses of the brain. For the most part, the brainways and their numerous synaptic connections perform their jobs over and over again. When neurons and brainways fail, new paths are sought.

Sometimes the failure isn't simply a breakdown in the synaptic connection but an increase or decrease in a chemical of the brain. This change in the brain chemistry can cause a variety of mental illnesses. People can begin thinking strange thoughts, seeing bizarre images that don't exist except in their minds, hear weird voices that no one else can hear, be certain that everyone is after them, or be afraid of everything around them. These kinds of mental illness have been lumped into a category called *schizophrenia*. Because of the great strides scientists have made in understanding the chemistry of the brain, some forms of schizophrenia can be controlled with drugs. Others, however, cannot.

Some mental illnesses are not caused solely by a chemical imbalance. In some cases, environment plays a part. This form of illness or mental breakdown can be related to high stress, great pressures to perform well in school or on the job, the loss of a parent, an abusive childhood, or the divorce of parents. These illnesses are usually treated by a psychiatrist, a doctor who is trained in understanding how the mind works. Though this therapy can last for years, these persons are normally not as ill as those suffering from schizophrenia.

Severe depression is another mental illness scientists believe is caused by a chemical problem in the brain. We all experience times when we are depressed. We feel sad, or lonely, or misunderstood. But these times usually pass. For those who are severely depressed, nothing helps but drug therapy. This severe condition is often brought on when the brain is not receiving certain chemical

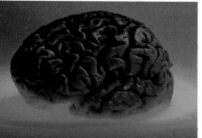

Side view of HUMAN BRAIN dramatic false coloring

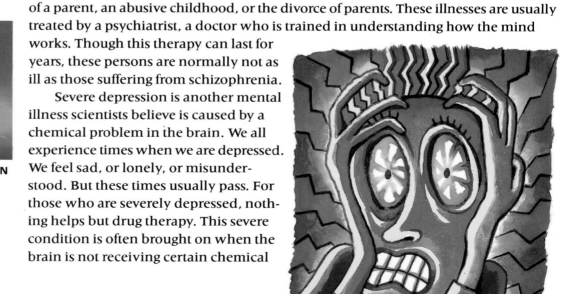

Brain

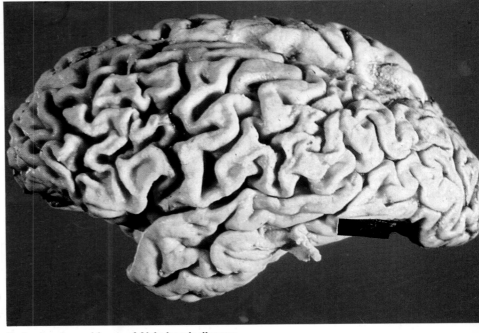

Brain showing evidence of Alzheimer's disease

transmitters or is receiving too much.

Other maladies of the brain are more physically crippling. Parkinson's disease affects the brain in such a way that it will not allow the body to move properly. Cerebral palsy also cripples and deforms the body. One disease of the brain on which a lot of research is being done is Alzheimer's disease. In this illness, the brainways between the cerebral cortex and the hippocampus have become tangled and twisted. The disease begins with a slight forgetfulness and progresses until the body eventually forgets to breathe. As with many diseases of the brain, there is no cure for Alzheimer's disease.

Even though scientists are beginning to understand the chemical imbalances that Alzheimer's patients experience, they are still struggling to understand why this occurs and how it can be reversed. The chemical that is not being properly produced acts as a messenger in the brain. Its message has something to do with the transfer of information and meaning. But before we can cure the disease, we have to understand more about the message it sends and how to read it.

Some maladies of the brain, like stroke, are not caused by a chemical problem but a physical one. A stroke is caused by a blockage in the blood vessels carrying blood and oxygen to the brain. The brain may make up only 5 percent of the body's weight, but it consumes nearly 20 percent of the body's oxygen, and when an adult brain is deprived of oxygen, it can experience serious damage or die. Many stroke victims who survive their strokes lose their ability to walk and talk. They then have to try to relearn these activities.

Probably the most common brain disorder affecting young people is injury: falling from a bike while not wearing a helmet, slipping while running around a pool, or being involved in a car accident while not wearing a seat belt. All of these injuries are preventable, so, PROTECT YOUR BRAIN. Wear a helmet while on a bike, and make sure everyone driving in the car with you buckles their seat belt. Another malady that can seriously injure your brain comes from taking "street drugs." The brain is a delicate instrument, one that can be damaged for life by just one mistake. Use it to think clearly before you act. When it comes to playing with the brain, the consequences are not worth the risk.

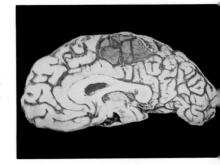

Section of brain showing an area of cerebral hemorrhage, or stroke (top, red)

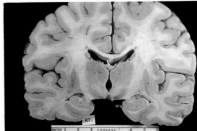

Cross section of brain displaying Parkinson's disease

A F T E R W O R D

THE HUMAN BRAIN is a remarkable system of parts, operating together and separately, to produce a healthy human being. We still know very little about how all its pieces fit together.

Maybe what you have read in this book will fire your imagination to learn more about the brain. And someday, your brain will help unravel the mysteries that have confused and inspired scientists from the time science was young.

BRAIN TEASER

Q: What do you get when you cross the brain of a cat with the brains of a 500 pound, three-headed monster?

A: I don't know, but if he asks for tuna, give it to him.

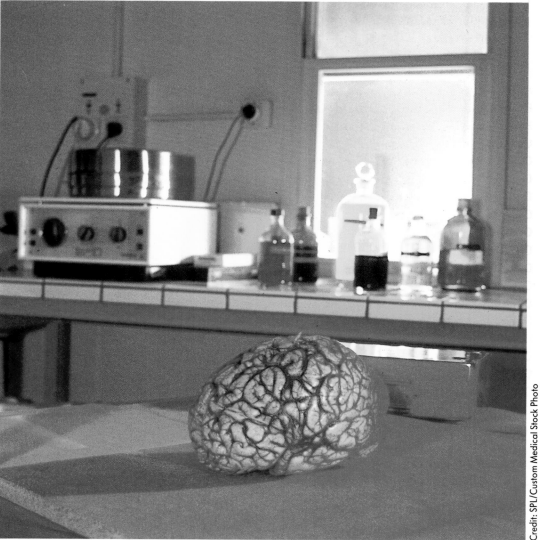

A postmortem specimen of a whole human brain sits on the table of a research laboratory.

Credit: SPL/Custom Medical Stock Photo

GLOSSARIZED INDEX

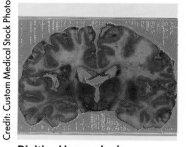

Credit: Custom Medical Stock Photo

Digitized human brain

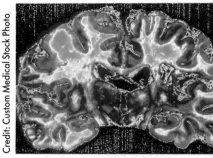

Credit: Custom Medical Stock Photo

Digitized section of the cerebellum

from John Muir Publications

X-ray Vision Series

Each title in the series is 8½" × 11", 48 pages, with four-color photographs and illustrations.

Looking Inside the Brain
Ron Schultz
$9.95 paper $14.95 hardcover

Looking Inside Cartoon Animation
Ron Schultz
$9.95 paper $14.95 hardcover

Looking Inside Sports Aerodynamics
Ron Schultz
$9.95 paper $14.95 hardcover

Masters of Motion Series

Each title in the series is 10¼" × 9", 48 pages, with four-color photographs and illustrations.

How to Drive an Indy Race Car
David Rubel
$9.95 paper $14.95 hardcover

How to Fly a 747
Tim Paulson
$9.95 paper $14.95 hardcover

How to Fly the Space Shuttle
Russell Shorto
$9.95 paper $14.95 hardcover

The Extremely Weird Series

All of the titles in the Extremely Weird Series are written by Sarah Lovett, are 8½" × 11", 48 pages, and $9.95 paperbacks.

Extremely Weird Bats
Extremely Weird Birds
Extremely Weird Endangered Species
Extremely Weird Fish
Extremely Weird Frogs
Extremely Weird Primates
Extremely Weird Reptiles
Extremely Weird Spiders

Other Titles of Interest

Kids Explore America's Hispanic Heritage
Westridge Young Writers Workshop
7" × 9", 112 pages, illustrations
$7.95 paper

Rads, Ergs, and Cheeseburgers
The Kids' Guide to Energy and the Environment
Bill Yanda
Illustrated by Michael Taylor
7" × 9", 108 pages, two-color illustrations
$12.95 paper

The Kids' Environment Book
What's Awry and Why
Anne Pedersen
Illustrated by Sally Blakemore
7" × 9", 192 pages, two-color illustrations
$13.95 paper
For Ages 10 and Up

The Indian Way
Learning to Communicate with Mother Earth
Gary McLain
Paintings by Gary McLain
Illustrations by Michael Taylor
7" × 9", 114 pages, two-color illustrations
$9.95 paper

The Quill Hedgehog Adventures Series

Green fiction for young readers. Each title in the series is written by John Waddington-Feather and illustrated by Doreen Edmond.

Quill's Adventures in the Great Beyond
Book One
5½" × 8½", 96 pages, $5.95 paper

Quill's Adventures in Wasteland
Book Two
5½" × 8½", 132 pages, $5.95 paper

Quill's Adventures in Grozzieland
Book Three
5½" × 8½", 132 pages, $5.95 paper

The Kidding Around Travel Series

All of the titles listed below are 64 pages and $9.95 except for *Kidding Around the National Parks of the Southwest* and *Kidding Around Spain*, which are 108 pages and $12.95.

Kidding Around Atlanta
Kidding Around Boston
Kidding Around Chicago
Kidding Around the Hawaiian Islands
Kidding Around London
Kidding Around Los Angeles
Kidding Around the National Parks
   of the Southwest
Kidding Around New York City
Kidding Around Paris
Kidding Around Philadelphia
Kidding Around San Diego
Kidding Around San Francisco
Kidding Around Santa Fe
Kidding Around Seattle
Kidding Around Spain
Kidding Around Washington, D.C.